J.C.

IN THE KITCHEN

John Contratti

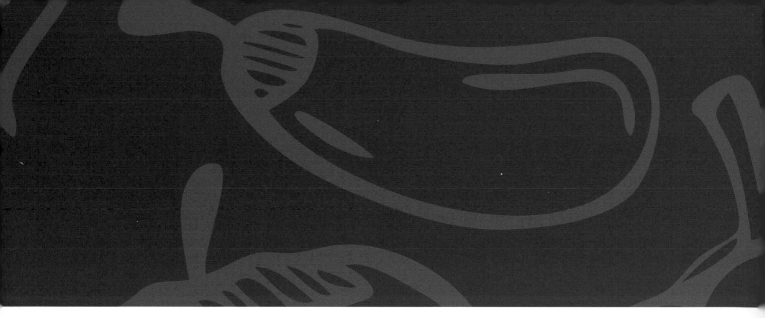

www.mascotbooks.com

J.C. in the Kitchen

Cover by Seth Miller.

For more information, please contact:
Mascot Books
620 Herndon Parkway, Suite 320
Herndon, VA 20170
info@mascotbooks.com

Library of Congress Control Number: 2021912820

CPSIA Code: PREG0821A
ISBN-13: 978-1-64543-939-4

Printed in China

FOR MY MOM, WHO ALWAYS SEEMS TO BE
COOKING SOMETHING.

CHICKEN

GRILLED CHICKEN AND SHRIMP WITH CITRUS SAUCE

A SIDE OF GUACAMOLE GOES WELL WITH THIS DISH.

DIRECTIONS

1. In a large skillet, put 2 tbs. of olive oil. Cook onions on medium heat until tender. Remove onions from skillet. Keep warm.

2. In the same skillet, add shrimp. Add a drop of olive oil, if needed. Sprinkle with sea salt and ground black pepper. Cook on each side for about 3 minutes. When done, remove and keep warm with onions.

3. In the same skillet, add 1 tbsp. of olive oil. Begin to cook chicken cutlets. Sprinkle with sea salt and ground black pepper. Cook on each side for about 4 minutes, depending on the thickness of the cutlets.

4. When cutlets are cooked, keep in skillet. Add shrimp and onions to skillet to heat through. Pour citrus sauce (see recipe, opposite) on top of the chicken and shrimp. When sauce begins to sizzle, remove and serve.

INGREDIENTS FOR CITRUS SAUCE

- 1 cup fresh orange juice
- 2 tbs. garlic (minced)
- 1 tbs. fresh rosemary (chopped)
- 2 tsp. butter
- 1 tsp. balsamic vinegar
- sea salt and ground black pepper (sprinkle of each)

YOU MAY WANT TO DOUBLE THIS RECIPE FOR EXTRA DIPPING.

DIRECTIONS FOR CITRUS SAUCE

1. Combine orange juice, garlic, and fresh rosemary in small saucepan. Bring to a boil over medium-high heat. Let simmer on low heat for 3 minutes. Add butter, vinegar, sea salt, and ground black pepper. Stir until the butter has melted. Serve warm and pour over shrimp and chicken.

LEMON CHICKEN FRANÇAISE

DIRECTIONS

1. Season 2 cups of flour with sea salt and ground black pepper.

2. Coat chicken cutlets in flour and shake off excess, then dip in egg.

3. Using a large skillet, heat vegetable oil.

4. Fry chicken for 4–5 minutes, or until golden brown on both sides. Remove chicken and set to the side.

5. Melt butter in the same skillet. Stir in 2 tbs. of flour. Stir well.

6. Add chicken broth and lemon juice. Simmer (low heat) until thickened (about 8–10 minutes).

7. Return chicken to the skillet. Continue simmering (low heat) until chicken is white in the center (about 10–12 minutes).

8. Serve chicken with parsley sprigs and lemon wedges.

INGREDIENTS

- 2 cups all-purpose flour plus 2 tbs.
- 1 lb. thin-sliced chicken cutlets
- 2 cups chicken broth
- 2 eggs (beaten)
- ½ cup butter
- ½ cup vegetable oil
- ½ cup fresh lemon juice
- fresh parsley sprigs
- 1 lemon (sliced)
- sea salt and ground black pepper

A REAL "CHICKEN CUTLET SANDWICH"

DIRECTIONS

1. Preheat oven to 350 degrees.

2. Fry bread cutlets in olive oil until golden brown. Drain on paper towels.

3. Using 2 cutlets like sliced bread, make a sandwich, layering ham, Muenster cheese, and tomatoes. Sprinkle a pinch of sea salt and ground black pepper.

4. After making the sandwiches, place them on a baking pan and bake for 5–7 minutes until cheese begins to melt.

5. Yields 4 sandwiches. Serve warm.

INGREDIENTS

- 8 chicken cutlet slices (breaded with seasoned crumbs and fried in olive oil until golden brown)
- ⅓ lb. Virginia ham (sliced thin)
- ⅓ lb. Muenster cheese (sliced thin)
- 8 slices of tomato (sliced thin)
- sea salt and ground black pepper

GRILLED CHICKEN WITH ASPARAGUS AND MUSHROOMS

INGREDIENTS

- 8 chicken cutlets (sliced)
- 2 cups white button mushrooms (sliced)
- 1 cup asparagus (ends trimmed)
- 2 cloves of garlic (chopped)
- olive oil
- sea salt and ground black pepper

DIRECTIONS

1. In a large skillet, put 2 tbs. of olive oil. Add garlic and let brown. Add mushrooms and asparagus. Cook for about 5 minutes, or until tender. Remove and put to the side.

2. Add an additional tbs. of olive oil. Cook chicken cutlets. Sprinkle with a pinch of sea salt and ground black pepper. When cutlets are just about cooked, return mushrooms and asparagus, and cook for an additional 2 minutes. Serve hot.

GRILLED CHICKEN WITH SPINACH, TOMATOES, AND OLIVES

DIRECTIONS

1. In a ziplock bag, add chicken cutlets, olive oil, balsamic vinegar, sea salt, and ground black pepper. Let marinate in refrigerator for at least 1 hour.

2. Grill chicken cutlets on both sides until done. Keep warm.

3. In a large skillet, add 2 tbs. of olive oil. Add garlic. Let brown for 1 minute. Add tomatoes and spinach. Sprinkle a pinch of sea salt. Stir. Add cooked cutlets to the pan.

4. Cook for an additional 3 minutes (heat through). Serve hot.

INGREDIENTS

- 6 chicken cutlets
- 1 lb. fresh spinach
- 1 cup cherry tomatoes (cut in half)
- 1 cup black olives (pits removed and sliced)
- 1 clove of garlic (chopped)
- 3 tbs. olive oil
- 2 tbs. balsamic vinegar
- 1 tsp. sea salt
- 1 tsp. ground black pepper
- 2 tbs. olive oil

CHICKEN BRUSCHETTA

DIRECTIONS

1. Put 2 tbs. of olive oil in a skillet. When oil heats, put in garlic. When garlic browns, add 1 tbs. of balsamic vinegar. Stir with a spoon. Add chicken cutlets to the pan. Cook on each side for 5–7 minutes, depending on thickness of the cutlets. You can add another tbs. of olive oil, if needed. Cut the chicken to see that it is white in the middle. Remove chicken and keep covered.

2. In a bowl, add tomatoes and onions. Sprinkle with a pinch of sea salt and ground black pepper. Add 1 tsp. of olive oil and 1 tsp. of balsamic vinegar. Mix well.

3. Preheat oven to 400 degrees. Get a baking pan. Coat the bottom of the pan with 1 tbs. of olive oil. Place chicken cutlets in pan. Put a slice of mozzarella on each cutlet. Spoon tomato mixture evenly on top of all cutlets. Bake in oven for 5–7 minutes, or until mozzarella melts. Serve warm.

INGREDIENTS

- 4 thick chicken cutlets (½ inch thick)
- 4 slices fresh mozzarella cheese
- 2 vine tomatoes (diced)
- 1 small red onion (chopped)
- 1 clove of garlic (chopped)
- 4 tbs. olive oil
- balsamic vinegar
- sea salt and ground black pepper

CHICKEN PARMESAN WITH ROASTED CHERRY TOMATOES

DIRECTIONS

1. Preheat oven to 400 degrees.

2. Sprinkle sea salt and ground black pepper on both sides of chicken cutlets. In a skillet, put 2 tbs. of olive oil. Brown chicken cutlets on each side for about 3 minutes. Remove from skillet.

3. In a baking pan, put 2 tbs. of olive oil. Bake cutlets for 25 minutes. Remove from oven and put fresh mozzarella slices on top. Return to oven for 5–8 minutes, or until cheese melts. Chicken should be white on the inside when done.

4. In a skillet, put 2 tbs. of olive oil. Brown garlic. Add cherry tomatoes, sun-dried tomatoes, red pepper flakes (optional), and parsley. Cook for about 5 minutes. Pour on top of chicken cutlets and serve.

INGREDIENTS

- 4 large boneless chicken breasts (about ½ inch thick)
- 2 dozen cherry tomatoes (cut in half)
- ½ cup sun-dried tomatoes in olive oil (chopped)
- 4 slices fresh mozzarella (¼ inch slices)
- 1 garlic clove (chopped)
- ½ tsp. red pepper flakes (optional)
- ½ tsp. dry parsley
- 2 tbs. olive oil
- sea salt and ground black pepper

GRILLED CHICKEN WITH DICED TOMATOES OVER SPINACH

DIRECTIONS

1. In a medium-sized pot, add 2 tbs. of olive oil. Add half of the chopped garlic. Cook for about 30 seconds. Add plum tomatoes and basil. Drizzle a little olive oil on top. Sprinkle sea salt and ground black pepper. Stir and cook on a medium-low heat until tomatoes are soft.

2. While tomatoes are simmering, take a large skillet. Coat skillet with olive oil (about 3 tbs.). Cook chicken cutlets. Sprinkle sea salt. Cook cutlets on each side for about 3–4 minutes each, depending on the thickness of cutlets. Keep cutlets warm when done.

3. In a large skillet, add remaining garlic and 2 tbs. of olive oil. Sauté garlic for a minute. Add spinach. Sprinkle with sea salt and ground black pepper. Stir spinach—it cooks quickly.

4. When spinach is soft, place on platter. Spoon some plum tomatoes on top. Put chicken cutlets on top of spinach. Spoon remaining plum tomatoes over chicken cutlets. Serve hot.

INGREDIENTS

- 8 chicken cutlets
- 6 plum tomatoes (diced)
- 3 cloves of garlic (chopped)
- ¼ cup fresh basil (chopped)
- 5 cups fresh spinach (rinsed and drained)
- olive oil
- sea salt and ground black pepper

HOMEMADE SESAME CHICKEN

DIRECTIONS

1. Place the eggs, sea salt, and ground black pepper in a bowl. Stir to combine.

2. Place the flour and ½ cup of cornstarch on a plate. Stir to combine.

3. Dip each piece of chicken into the egg mixture, then into the flour. Repeat the process with each piece of chicken.

4. Heat about 3 inches of oil in a deep pan.

5. When oil begins to sizzle, add pieces of chicken to the pan. Cook for 5 minutes, or until crispy and golden brown. Repeat the process with the remaining chicken.

6. Drain the chicken on paper towels.

7. While the chicken is cooking, combine the honey, soy sauce, ketchup, brown sugar, rice vinegar, sesame oil, and 2 tsp. of cornstarch in a bowl.

8. Heat the teaspoon of oil in a large pan over medium heat. Add the garlic and cook for 30 seconds. Add the honey-sauce mixture and bring to a simmer. Cook for 3 minutes, or until the sauce has thickened.

9. Add the crispy chicken to the pan and toss to coat with the sauce. Sprinkle with sesame seeds and green onions. Serve hot.

SAUCE INGREDIENTS

- 1 tsp. vegetable oil
- 1 tsp. fresh garlic (minced)
- ¼ cup honey
- ⅓ cup soy sauce (reduced sodium, if possible)
- ½ cup ketchup
- 3 tbs. brown sugar
- ¼ cup rice vinegar
- 1 tbs. toasted sesame oil
- 2 tsp. cornstarch
- 2 tbs. sesame seeds
- 2 tbs. green onion (sliced)

INGREDIENTS

- 1 ½-lb. boneless, skinless chicken breast cut into 1-inch pieces.
- 2 eggs (beaten)
- sea salt and ground black pepper to taste
- ½ cup all-purpose flour
- ½ cup cornstarch
- vegetable oil for frying

CHICKEN AND RICE

DIRECTIONS

1. In a large pot, brown the onion and garlic in the olive oil. Add sea salt, pepper, oregano, and can of Del Monte sauce. Next, add olives. Simmer for 5 minutes.

2. Add water, chicken broth, and rice. The liquids should cover the rice.

3. Cook rice at a medium flame for about 30 minutes, or until rice starts to dry and become fluffy.

4. Roughly 5 minutes before the rice is done, add cooked chicken to rice. Make sure chicken is heated through.

5. Serve hot.

INGREDIENTS

- 1 cooked rotisserie chicken cut into bite-size pieces (no skin or bones)
- 2 cups brown rice
- 1 small onion (chopped)
- 2 garlic cloves (chopped)
- ½ cup pitted salad olives (Goya)
- 1 8-oz. can Del Monte sauce (or sauce of your choice)
- 2 cups water
- ½ cup olive oil
- 2 cups chicken broth
- 1 tsp. sea salt
- ½ tsp. oregano
- ground black pepper (to taste)

WALNUT CHICKEN

DIRECTIONS

1. Dip chicken breasts in egg whites.

2. In a bowl, mix walnuts and brown sugar. Dip chicken breasts into walnut mixture. Coat both sides.

3. In a large skillet, put 3 tbs. of vegetable oil.

4. When oil is heated, cook chicken breasts on both sides (time depends on thickness of breasts). Chicken should be white on the inside when sliced.

5. Optional: serve on lettuce.

DIPPING SAUCE (OPTIONAL)

- ¼ cup low-sodium soy sauce
- 3 tbs. brown sugar
- 3 scallions (chopped)
- Combine all ingredients in a bowl and use for dipping. If too salty, add more sugar. If too sweet, add an additional drop of soy sauce.

INGREDIENTS

- 4 large boneless, skinless chicken breasts
- 2 cups walnuts (finely chopped)
- ¼ cup brown sugar
- 2 egg whites (beaten)
- 3 tbs. vegetable oil plus extra, if needed

CHICKEN CUTLETS WITH PECAN SAUCE

AT A CERTAIN POINT, YOU WILL HAVE 2 SKILLETS WORKING AT THE SAME TIME.

DIRECTIONS

1. Boil carrots until tender and drain (about 12–15 minutes).

2. In a skillet, put 2 tbs. of olive oil. Cook zucchini until browned and tender. Set to the side.

3. Flour cutlets. Sprinkle with sea salt and ground black pepper.

4. In another skillet, put 1 tbs. of butter. Add pecans. Melt butter. Stir pecans for about 1 minute and remove.

5. Add ½ stick of butter. Cook cutlets on both sides until brown and well cooked. Remove cutlets and keep warm.

6. Add remaining butter to skillet. Melt. Add vegetable stock, brown sugar, and pecans. Stir well.

7. Add carrots to zucchini skillet. Heat through. Place carrots and zucchini on a platter. Place chicken on top. Pour pecan sauce on top of chicken.

INGREDIENTS

- 8 chicken cutlets
- 3 large zucchinis (cut into small pieces)
- 1 package baby carrots
- 1/2 cup pecans
- 1 stick of butter
- 1 tbs. flour
- 2 tbs. brown sugar
- 1 cup vegetable stock
- sea salt and ground black pepper
- 2 tbs. olive oil

SALADS & APPETIZERS

GRILLED STACKED TOMATOES

DIRECTIONS

1. Salt and pepper ears of corn. Brush with a little olive oil. Grill corn until it's a little browned. Remove and let cool. Once cooled, shuck the corn off the cob and place it to the side.

2. In a large skillet, cook bacon until crispy and remove. Let dry on a paper towel.

3. Brush olive oil on each tomato slice. Sprinkle a pinch of salt and pepper on each side. Grill tomatoes on each side for about 5 minutes. Tomatoes should be a little tender, not soft.

4. To stack tomatoes, take a tomato slice and place an avocado slice on top. Repeat step.

5. On the top, place two slices of bacon and a slice of avocado. Put 2 tbs. of corn on top.

6. In a small bowl, mix 2 tbs. of olive oil, 1 tbs. of balsamic vinegar, and 1/2 tsp. of parsley. Stir. Drizzle a little over tomato and serve.

7. Yields 4 stacks.

INGREDIENTS

- 3 large beefsteak tomatoes (cut 4 slices out of each tomato)
- 3 ripe avocados (sliced)
- 8 slices of bacon
- 2 ears of corn
- sea salt and ground black pepper
- ½ tsp. fresh parsley (chopped)
- olive oil
- balsamic vinegar

FRESH MOZZARELLA AND TOMATOES WITH ROASTED GARLIC

DIRECTIONS

1. Preheat oven to 400 degrees.

2. Take 1 bulb of garlic and place it on aluminum foil. Sprinkle with a little olive oil and sea salt. Wrap up and bake in oven for 30 minutes. Remove and let cool.

3. On a platter, place sliced tomatoes and mozzarella. Sprinkle chopped basil and a little sea salt on top (see photo).

4. In a food processor, mix olive oil and cooked garlic (3 cloves). Beat for about 1 minute.

5. Drizzle olive oil over tomatoes and fresh mozzarella. You can put remaining cooked garlic cloves on top.

INGREDIENTS

- 2 whole tomatoes (sliced; keep refrigerated)
- 1 lb. fresh mozzarella (sliced)
- 5 basil leaves (chopped)
- sea salt
- 5 tbs. olive oil
- 3 garlic cloves (cooked)

SHRIMP AND FETA HORS D'OEUVRES

DIRECTIONS

1. In a large bowl, mix all ingredients except phyllo shells.

2. Fill shells with mixture (see photo).

INGREDIENTS

- 16 large shrimp (boiled, tails removed; chopped)
- ½ cup fresh arugula (chopped)
- ½ cup feta cheese (chopped)
- ½ cup grape tomatoes (chopped)
- 2 tbs. olive oil
- ½ tsp. sea salt
- 2 dozen mini phyllo shells (room temperature)

GRILLED CHICKEN ESCAROLE SALAD WITH FRESH MOZZARELLA

USE A DRESSING OF YOUR CHOICE OR USE A LITTLE OLIVE OIL AND LEMON JUICE ON TOP.

DIRECTIONS

1. Marinate chicken cutlets in olive oil, lemon juice, and sea salt. Let marinate for at least 1 hour refrigerated.

2. Grill cutlets on both sides for about 4–6 minutes. Let cool and slice into thin pieces.

3. In a large bowl, place escarole. Place sliced chicken cutlets, sliced mozzarella, chickpeas, marinated mushrooms, and tomatoes on top.

INGREDIENTS

- 1 lb. fresh escarole (rinsed, drained, and chopped)
- 4 chicken cutlets
- 2 tomatoes (sliced)
- 1 lb. fresh mozzarella (sliced)
- 1 cup chickpeas
- 1 cup marinated mushrooms
- 1 tbs. olive oil
- 1 lemon (juiced)
- 1 tsp. sea salt

COLD TORTELLINI SPINACH SALAD WITH APPLES AND STRAWBERRIES

DIRECTIONS

1. Boil tortellini to desired taste. Let cool.

2. On a platter, place spinach. Put all other ingredients on top (see photo).

3. Drizzle your favorite vinaigrette dressing on top and serve.

INGREDIENTS

- 1 10-oz. bag of cheese tortellini
- 2 apples (sliced)
- 1 ½ cups sliced strawberries
- 2 cups fresh spinach
- ¼ cup scallions (chopped)
- ½ cup toasted pine nuts (pignoli nut)

ARUGULA TOMATO SALAD WITH FRIED FETA

DIRECTIONS

1. Dip feta cheese in egg and then breadcrumbs.

2. In a skillet, put 2 tbs. of olive oil. When heated, add feta cheese. Cook on both sides for a minute each. Remove from skillet.

3. On a large platter, spread out arugula, tomatoes, red onion, and olives (see photo).

4. Mix salad dressing ingredients. Drizzle over salad. Put fried feta on top.

DRESSING

- 3 tbs. olive oil
- ½ lemon (juiced)
- 2 tsp. chopped fresh oregano
- 1 ½ tbs. honey
- pinch of ground black pepper

INGREDIENTS

- 4 tomatoes (sliced)
- 1 small red onion (thinly sliced)
- 2 cups fresh arugula (rinsed and dried)
- 1 small can pitted black olives (drained)
- 8 oz. feta cheese (cut into cubes)
- 1 egg (beaten)
- 1 cup seasoned breadcrumbs
- 2 tbs. olive oil

SHRIMP BALLS

YOU CAN ALSO BAKE IN A 350-DE-GREE OVEN FOR ABOUT 20 MINUTES, OR UNTIL GOLDEN BROWN.

DIRECTIONS

1. Boil 4 cups of water and add rice. Bring to a boil and lower heat. Once rice absorbs water and is fluffy, remove from heat. Set rice to the side when done.

2. Heat skillet with 2 tbs. vegetable oil. Add onion and brown lightly.

3. Add shrimp and tomato sauce. Add a pinch of sea salt and ground black pepper.

4. With skillet uncovered, add peas and let tomato sauce reduce.

5. Once mixture has thickened, put to the side and let cool.

6. In a large bowl, mix rice with 4 eggs, mozzarella, and Parmesan cheese.

7. Add shrimp and pea mixture. Mix well by hand. With hands, shape rice into a medium ball.

8. Once shrimp balls are molded tightly, put them on a sheet pan.

9. Refrigerate for about 30 minutes.

10. Beat remaining 4 eggs in a bowl.

11. Take rice balls from refrigerator, dip them into the eggs, and then roll in breadcrumbs.

YOU CAN MAKE THEM SMALLER FOR HORS D'OEUVRES.

INGREDIENTS

- 1 medium sweet onion (chopped)
- 2 cups cooked shrimp (chopped)
- 1 cup green peas
- 1 cup tomato sauce
- sea salt and ground black pepper
- 1 cup vegetable oil plus extra (You can use olive oil.)
- 2 cups white rice
- 4 cups water
- 8 eggs
- breadcrumbs (plain or seasoned)
- 2 cups mozzarella (grated)
- 1 cup Parmesan cheese (grated)

12. Return to refrigerator and allow to set for another 20 minutes.

13. Heat 1 quart of oil in large, deep saucepan. With a large, slotted spoon, gently place shrimp balls in hot oil.

14. Cook until golden brown on all sides. Let drain on paper towels.

15. Yields approximately 15 rice balls.

EGGPLANT CAPONATA

DIRECTIONS

1. Peel and cube eggplant. Cut pepper and onion into small bite-size pieces. Slice mushrooms.

2. In a skillet, put 3 tbs. of olive oil. Add garlic. Then add eggplant, peppers, onions, and mushrooms. Cover and cook for about 10 minutes. Stir frequently. Add a drop more oil, if needed.

3. Add all the remaining ingredients (green olives, tomato paste, water, wine vinegar, sugar, oregano, and salt—ground pepper to taste).

4. Stir everything together. On a low heat, simmer for 30 minutes until eggplant is tender.

5. Refrigerate overnight. Serve cold. Keeps in refrigerator for 1 week. Serve on toasted bread or on your favorite cracker.

INGREDIENTS

- 1 large eggplant
- 1 large sweet onion
- 1 large green pepper
- 1 cup fresh white button mushrooms
- 3 garlic cloves (crushed)
- ½ cup stuffed green olives (with pimentos)
- 1 6-oz. can tomato paste
- ¼ cup water
- 2 tbs. wine vinegar
- 1 ½ tsp. sugar
- 1 tsp. oregano
- 1 tsp. sea salt
- olive oil
- freshly ground black pepper to taste

FRIED GREEN TOMATOES

YOU CAN ALSO SERVE WITH A LITTLE MARINARA SAUCE.

INGREDIENTS

- 3 green tomatoes (sliced)
- 1 cup panko breadcrumbs
- 1 cup grated Parmesan cheese
- 3 egg whites (beaten)
- olive oil
- sea salt

DIRECTIONS

1. Mix breadcrumbs and grated Parmesan cheese in a bowl. Put egg whites in a bowl.

2. Dip tomatoes in egg whites. Next, dip in breadcrumb mixture.

3. In a large skillet, put 4 tbs. of olive oil. Cook tomatoes on both sides until tender and crisp. Add more olive oil, if needed, while cooking. Dry on paper towels.

4. Sprinkle with a little sea salt.

STUFFED ARTICHOKE HEARTS

DIRECTIONS

1. Preheat oven to 350 degrees.

2. In a large bowl, mix breadcrumbs, Parmesan cheese, pignoli nuts, prosciutto, ground black pepper, parsley, and 3 tbs. of olive oil. Mix well. If breadcrumbs are still a little dry, add 1 tsp. of olive oil. Mix well.

3. Stuff each artichoke heart (see photo).

4. In deep baking dish, coat the bottom with 1 tbs. of olive oil. You can lightly brush the artichoke hearts with a little olive oil. Stand up all artichoke hearts and bake in oven for 12 minutes, or until breadcrumbs are slightly browned.

5. Serve hot.

INGREDIENTS

- 2 or 3 cans of whole artichoke hearts (drained; usually about 8 hearts in a can)
- 1 cup plain breadcrumbs
- 1 cup grated Parmesan cheese
- ½ cup pignoli nuts
- 6 slices of prosciutto (chopped)
- 1 tbs. fresh parsley (chopped)
- ¼ tsp. ground black pepper
- 3 tbs. olive oil plus extra, if needed

MEAT

SHREDDED GINGER PORK WITH MIXED VEGETABLES

DIRECTIONS

1. Using 2 tbs. of sesame oil, cook pork strips in a large skillet (about 5 minutes). Remove and put to the side.

2. In same skillet, put 3 tbs. of sesame oil. Heat up for a minute and add garlic, red onions, carrots, mushrooms, string beans, and snow peas. Stir frequently. Add 2 tbs. of soy sauce and stir. If you need a little more sesame oil, add a little.

3. When vegetables are tender, add cooked pork, basil, and ginger. Drizzle 1 drop of sesame oil and 1 tbs. of soy sauce. Cook on high heat for 3 minutes and continue to stir.

4. Serve hot.

INGREDIENTS

- 10 pork cutlets (cut in strips)
- 1 medium red onion (sliced)
- 2 garlic cloves (chopped)
- 2 cups fresh snap peas
- 1 cup carrots (shredded into small pieces)
- 1 cup white button mushrooms (rinsed and dried)
- 1 cup string beans (rinsed and cut in half)
- 2 tbs. fresh ginger (shredded)
- 5 tbs. sesame oil
- 3 tbs. soy sauce (low sodium)
- 1 tbs. fresh basil (chopped)

BARBECUE-SEASONED PORK CHOPS WITH SAUTÉED SHIITAKE MUSHROOMS

DIRECTIONS

1. In a bowl, mix sea salt, garlic powder, and thyme.

2. Coat pork chops with a little olive oil. Sprinkle mixed seasoning on chops.

3. Grill chops about 12–15 minutes. Frequently turn. Pork should be white on the inside when done.

4. In a large skillet, put 2 tbs. of olive oil. Add garlic and brown for 1 minute. Add mushrooms. Sauté for about 5 minutes, or until tender. Sprinkle with a pinch of sea salt.

INGREDIENTS

- 4 boneless pork chops
- 1 lb. shiitake mushrooms (sliced)
- 2 garlic cloves (chopped)
- 2 tbs. olive oil plus extra, if needed
- 2 tsp. sea salt
- 1 tsp. garlic powder
- 1 tsp. thyme

SHEPHERD'S PIE

DIRECTIONS

1. Wash and peel potatoes. Cut potatoes into cubes and put in boiling water for about 25 minutes, or until potatoes are soft. Drain potatoes well. In a bowl, add potatoes, cream, butter, and a little sea salt and ground black pepper. With a mixer, mix until creamy and set to the side.

2. In a skillet, put 2 tbs. of olive oil. Add onions and red peppers. Cook for about 3 minutes and add ground beef and a pinch of salt and pepper. Brown beef until cooked (about 10 minutes). Add peas and drizzle some olive oil on top. Stir thoroughly.

3. In a baking pan, drizzle a little olive oil at the bottom of the pan. First, put a layer of creamy potatoes. Next, pour the meat mixture on top. Finally, cover with another layer of creamy potatoes. Drizzle a little olive oil on top. Sprinkle salt, pepper, and paprika (optional) on top.

4. Put baking pan in a 350-degree oven for 20 minutes. Potatoes should be a little browned on top.

INGREDIENTS

- 2 lbs. white potatoes (your choice)
- 1 lb. ground beef
- 1 8-oz. can of peas (drained)
- 1 red pepper (diced)
- 1 small onion (chopped)
- 1 cup heavy cream
- ½ stick butter or margarine
- 2 tbs. olive oil plus a little extra
- sea salt and ground black pepper
- paprika (optional)

VEAL WITH TOMATOES AND MUSHROOMS

DIRECTIONS

1. In a large skillet, melt butter. Once melted, add veal cutlets. Season with a pinch of sea salt on each piece. Cook on both sides for about 3–4 minutes each. Remove and set to the side.

2. In the same skillet, add olive oil and garlic. Brown for a minute. Add mushrooms, tomatoes, and sun-dried tomatoes. Cook for about 10 minutes. Sprinkle with sea salt.

3. When tomatoes are tender, return cutlets to the pan. Raise the heat high for 3 minutes.

4. Serve on a platter with basil on top.

INGREDIENTS

- 8 slices of veal cutlets
- 2 cups of white button mushrooms (sliced)
- 1 cup cherry tomatoes (sliced)
- ½ cup sun-dried tomatoes (chopped)
- 5 pieces of basil (chopped into pieces)
- 2 cloves of garlic (sliced)
- sea salt
- 2 tbs. olive oil
- 3 tbs. butter

VEAL PICCATA

DIRECTIONS

1. In a large bowl, add 1 cup of flour, 1 tsp. of sea salt, and 1 tsp. of ground black pepper. Mix together. Coat both sides of each cutlet in flour. Shake off the excess flour.

2. In a skillet, add 2 tbs. of olive oil. Once oil heats, add 2 tbs. of butter. Cook veal until golden brown (2 minutes on each side). Remove cutlets from skillet and keep covered.

3. In the same skillet, add 1 cup of dry white wine and bring to a boil. When half of the wine is reduced, add chicken stock, garlic, capers, lemon juice, and pepperoncini. Cook for about 5 minutes, or until sauce becomes thick. Add ½ tsp. of sea salt and remaining butter. Stir thoroughly. Add parsley. When butter has melted, return cutlets to skillet. Warm for another 4 minutes (2 minutes on each side).

INGREDIENTS

- 8 slices of veal cutlets
- 1 cup flour
- 1 cup dry white wine
- 6 tbs. butter
- ½ cup chicken stock
- 1 garlic clove (chopped)
- 1 lemon (juiced)
- 4 tbs. capers
- 2 pepperoncini (chopped)
- 1 tbs. chopped parsley
- 2 tbs. olive oil
- sea salt and ground black pepper

FETA GREEK PORK CHOPS

DIRECTIONS

1. Put a tbs. of olive oil in a skillet. Cook leeks until tender and a little crispy. Set to the side.

2. In a large skillet, or on a grill, put 1 tbs. of olive oil. Cook pork chops on each side. Depending on the thickness, cook at least a total of 10–12 minutes. Chops should be white when you slice into them. Sprinkle with a pinch of sea salt and ground black pepper.

3. When chops are just about done, add cooked leeks and feta cheese on top of chops. Cook 1 additional minute and then serve.

4. Serve warm.

INGREDIENTS

- 4 boneless pork chops
- 1 cup fresh leeks (chopped)
- 1 cup feta cheese
- 3 tbs. olive oil
- sea salt
- ground black pepper

BASIL FLANK STEAK

DIRECTIONS

1. In a large skillet, add olive oil and garlic. Brown garlic and then add flank steak. Add 1 tsp. of sea salt. Cook for about 5 minutes, stirring frequently. When cooked, remove and put to the side, covered.

2. In the same skillet, add 3 tbs. of sesame oil. Add mushrooms and carrots. Stir frequently. When tender, add basil. Stir well.

3. Add cooked flank steak to the pan and add 1 tbs. of sesame oil. Add 1 tsp. of sea salt. Mix together and cook for an additional two minutes and serve.

4. Serve hot.

INGREDIENTS

- 2 lbs. flank steak (thinly sliced)
- 1 lb. white button mushrooms (washed and sliced)
- ½ lb. carrots (sliced thin)
- 3 tbs. basil (chopped)
- 2 garlic cloves (chopped)
- 3 tbs. olive oil
- 4 tbs. sesame oil
- 2 tsp. sea salt

CORNED BEEF AND EGG HERO WITH ROASTED GARLIC PEPPERS

DIRECTIONS

1. Slice peppers and remove seeds.

2. In a large skillet, put olive oil. Brown garlic for 1 minute and add peppers. Cook until tender. Add a little more oil if needed.

3. In a separate skillet, melt butter. When butter has melted, add eggs, corned beef sea salt and ground black pepper. Cook eggs until your desired taste.

4. Put eggs on hero bread and serve with a side of roasted peppers.

5. Yields 4 heroes.

INGREDIENTS

- 1 dozen eggs (beat eggs until fluffy)
- ½ lb. cooked corned beef (chopped)
- 3 tbs. butter
- 1 tsp. sea salt
- 1 tsp. ground black pepper
- 2 red bell peppers
- 2 orange bell peppers
- 2 yellow bell peppers
- 2 garlic cloves (chopped)
- 3 tbs. olive oil

BEEF BURGUNDY

SERVE WITH A GREEN SIDE VEGE-TABLE. I RECOMMEND SAUTEÉD ARU-GULA AND CHICKPEAS IN OLIVE OIL.

DIRECTIONS

1. In a large skillet, over high heat, cook the bacon until it turns crisp. Leave to the side.

2. Pour all but 2 tbs. of bacon grease from the pan.

3. Sauté the onions and celery in the bacon grease for 5 minutes, or until the vegetables turn soft.

4. Transfer vegetables to a bowl and set to the side.

5. Season the beef with sea salt and ground black pepper, and brown it in the remaining bacon grease. Once all sides of the beef are browned, sprinkle the parsley, thyme, rosemary, allspice, and flour over the beef.

6. Stir in the tomato paste and cook beef for 1 minute.

7. Add cooked vegetables, crisped bacon, wine, and beef stock into the pan with the beef, and then cook the mixture over low heat, covered, for about 1 hour to 1 hour and 15 minutes.

8. Beef burgundy is done when the meat and vegetables are tender, and the sauce is thickened.

INGREDIENTS

- 5 slices bacon (chopped)
- 1 ½ cups pearl onions
- ¼ cup celery (finely chopped)
- 2 lbs. beef chuck (cubed)
- ½ tsp. sea salt
- ¼ tsp. ground black pepper
- 2 tsp. dried parsley
- ½ tsp. dried thyme
- ¼ tsp. dried crushed rosemary
- 1/16 tsp. ground allspice (pinch)
- 1 tbs. all-purpose flour
- 1 tsp. tomato paste
- 1 ¼ cups burgundy wine or a dry red wine
- ¾ cup beef stock

SAUSAGE AND ZUCCHINI

DIRECTIONS

1. In a large skillet, add 3 tbs. of olive oil. Add garlic and let brown. Add zucchini. Add a pinch of sea salt and ground black pepper. Stir. Cook for about 7–10 minutes, or until zucchini is tender. Remove from skillet.

2. In another skillet, add 1 tbs. of olive oil. Cook sausage for about 10 minutes. You can add a little more olive oil if needed. Sausage should be cooked well. Add zucchini and mix well. Add an additional tsp. of sea salt, if needed. Stir together. Cook for an additional 2 minutes and serve.

INGREDIENTS

- 1 lb. sweet or hot sausage (sliced into bite-size pieces)
- 3 medium zucchinis (cut into bite-size pieces)
- 3 garlic cloves (chopped)
- 4 tbs. olive oil
- sea salt and ground black pepper

CHEDDAR BURGERS WITH SPINACH AND CARROTS

AS A SUGGESTION, PUT GUACAMOLE ON TOP.

DIRECTIONS

1. In a large bowl, mix all ingredients.

2. Form meat into burgers.

3. Cook to desired taste.

INGREDIENTS

- 1 ½ lbs. ground beef
- 1 cup fresh spinach (chopped)
- 1 cup fresh carrots (minced)
- 1 cup white cheddar cheese (grated)
- 1 tsp. sea salt
- ½ tsp. ground black pepper

BRACIOLE

DIRECTIONS

1. On each slice of meat, sprinkle a pinch of sea salt, ground black pepper, garlic, and parsley.

2. Put slices of hard-boiled egg and mozzarella on top.

3. Roll cutlets tightly, and tie with twine or thread. In a large pan, put olive oil. Cook braciole on all sides for about 15 minutes. Remove from pan.

4. Cook braciole in a pot of tomato sauce for 2 hours on a low heat. Braciole should be covered in sauce. There should be enough sauce in a deep pot. Remove twine or thread.

5. Serve hot.

INGREDIENTS

- 1 lb. London broil (sliced into thin cutlets; about 8–10 slices)
- 1 lb. fresh mozzarella (sliced)
- 6 hard-boiled eggs (sliced)
- ¼ cup chopped parsley
- ½ cup grated Parmesan cheese
- 2 garlic cloves of garlic (chopped)
- 4 tbs. olive oil
- sea salt and ground black pepper
- tomato sauce (enough to cover meat in pot)

SEAFOOD

PARMESAN TILAPIA

DIRECTIONS

1. Rinse tilapia in cold water and let dry on paper towels.

2. Mix egg whites in a bowl.

3. In another bowl, mix breadcrumbs, Parmesan cheese, parsley, and ground black pepper.

4. Dip tilapia in egg whites and then coat in breadcrumbs on both sides.

5. In a large skillet, add olive oil. Fry tilapia on each side for about 4 minutes each. Tilapia should be crispy on both sides. Fish should be white and flaky on the inside.

INGREDIENTS

- 4 large slices of tilapia
- 1 cup breadcrumbs
- ½ cup grated Parmesan cheese
- 1 tsp. dry parsley
- 1 tsp. ground black pepper
- 3 egg whites (beaten)
- 4 tbs. olive oil

GRILLED SHRIMP, ZUCCHINI, AND PEPPERS

SERVE WITH FRESH LEMON AND TZATZIKI SAUCE

DIRECTIONS

1. Rub 3 tbs. of olive oil on grill. Heat grill before placing vegetables and shrimp on grill. Aluminum foil on grill grates can prevent vegetables and shrimp from falling through.

2. Place shrimp, zucchini, and red bell peppers on grill. Brush a little olive oil on top. Sprinkle with thyme, sea salt, and ground black pepper.

3. 3. Turn over after about 3–4 minutes. Check frequently so nothing is burnt. Note that shrimp cooks a little faster than the vegetables. After turning over, brush with olive oil and sprinkle with thyme, sea salt, and ground black pepper. Cook for an additional 3 minutes. Remove from grill and serve.

INGREDIENTS

- 1 lb. medium shrimp (cleaned and thawed)
- 3 large zucchinis (sliced)
- 5 red bell peppers (cut into small squares)
- 3 tbs. olive oil, plus extra for brushing
- 2 tsp. dry thyme
- sea salt and ground black pepper

BAKED FETA SHRIMP

DIRECTIONS

1. Open can of tomatoes. Slice tomatoes.

2. In a large skillet, put 2 tbs. of olive oil. Cook garlic and shallots for about 5 minutes.

3. Add tomatoes. Sprinkle with sea salt and ground black pepper. Cook for 10 minutes.

4. Make sure uncooked shrimp are dry and not wet. In a bowl, put shrimp. Add 1 tbs. of olive oil and a pinch of sea salt. Mix well.

5. In a round baking casserole dish, coat the bottom with a little olive oil. Add cooked tomatoes evenly on the bottom.

6. Put uncooked shrimp on top. Sprinkle feta cheese on top (see photo).

7. In a preheated 400-degree oven, bake shrimp for about 10–12 minutes.

8. Serve hot.

INGREDIENTS

- 1 lb. uncooked medium shrimp (about 20 pieces)
- 1 large can tomatoes (whole pieces)
- 1 cup feta cheese (crumbled)
- 2 garlic cloves (chopped)
- 2 small shallots (chopped)
- 3 tbs. olive oil plus a little extra
- sea salt and ground black pepper

FARFALLE SHRIMP AND SCALLOPS IN DRY WHITE WINE

DIRECTIONS

1. In a large skillet, put 3 tbs. of olive oil and garlic. Brown garlic for 1 minute and add shrimp and scallops.

2. Stir and turn frequently. Sprinkle with sea salt and ground black pepper.

3. After 4–5 minutes, add dry white wine. Stir.

4. Make sure your pasta is drained well, and place it in a bowl.

5. Pour scallops and shrimp on top. Sprinkle parsley and Parmesan cheese on top.

INGREDIENTS

- 1 lb. farfalle (cooked to your desired taste)
- 1 lb. medium shrimp (cleaned and thawed)
- 1 lb. bay scallops
- 3 garlic cloves (chopped)
- 1 cup dry white wine
- 3 tbs. olive oil
- 2 tsp. sea salt
- 1 tsp. ground black pepper
- 2 tsp. dry parsley (fresh)
- ¼ cup Parmesan cheese

SCALLOPS AND GARLIC BRUSSELS SPROUTS

SQUEEZE LEMON ON TOP.

DIRECTIONS

1. In a large skillet, put 3 tbs. of olive oil and garlic. Sauté for 1 minute. Add Brussels sprouts. Sprinkle with sea salt and ground black pepper. Stir. Add vegetable stock. Cook and stir frequently for about 10 minutes. Remove and set to the side.

2. In the same skillet, add 1 tbs. of olive oil. Add scallops. Sprinkle with sea salt and ground black pepper. Cook on each side for 2–3 minutes each.

3. Add cooked Brussels sprouts to scallops. Mix well for 1 minute.

4. Serve hot.

INGREDIENTS

- 1 ½ lb. sea scallops
- ¾ lb. Brussels sprouts (cut into quarters)
- 1 cup vegetable stock
- 4 garlic cloves (chopped)
- 4 tbs. olive oil
- sea salt and ground black pepper

BROWN RICE WITH SHRIMP, ARUGULA, AND CARROTS

A LITTLE LEMON SQUEEZED ON TOP IS OPTIONAL

DIRECTIONS

1. Boil thawed shrimp for 5 minutes and drain. Set to the side.

2. In a pot, put rice and vegetable stock. Bring to a boil. When it begins to boil, set to a medium heat. In approximately 10 minutes, rice should absorb vegetable stock. Keep an eye on it. Once most of the liquid has been absorbed, remove from heat.

3. In a large skillet, pour olive oil. Add shallots, garlic, and carrots. Sprinkle with sea salt and ground black pepper. Stir frequently. When carrots are soft, add shrimp and arugula.

4. Mix together. Arugula should cook quickly. Add 1 additional tbs. of olive oil, if needed. Sprinkle a little more sea salt and ground black pepper.

5. Get a large bowl. Place brown rice in bowl. Pour shrimp mixture on top of rice and mix together.

INGREDIENTS

- 2 cups brown rice
- 4 cups vegetable stock
- ½ lb. small shrimp (thawed)
- 3 carrots (sliced into thin circles)
- 2 cups fresh arugula (rinsed and drained)
- 2 shallots chopped
- 2 garlic cloves
- 4 tbs. olive oil (extra tbs., if needed)
- sea salt and ground black pepper

FILET OF SOLE HERO TOPPED WITH SHRIMP TOMATO SALAD

DIRECTIONS

1. Dip sole into egg and then breadcrumbs. Coat well.

2. In a large skillet, put about 3 tbs. of olive oil. Cook sole on both sides for about 3 minutes each. Let drain on paper towel.

3. In a large bowl, put tomatoes, red onions, shrimp, 1 tbs. of olive oil, and white balsamic vinegar and sea salt. Mix well.

4. Place filet of sole on hero bread. Top with shrimp tomato salad.

INGREDIENTS

- 4 large slices of filet of sole
- 1 cup seasoned breadcrumbs
- 1 egg (beaten)
- olive oil (for frying)
- 4 hero breads
- ½ cup red onion (sliced)
- 2 tomatoes (cut into small pieces)
- 16 small shrimp (boiled and cooled)
- 1 tsp. sea salt
- 4 tbs. olive oil
- 1 tbs. white balsamic vinegar

BAKED SALMON TERIYAKI

DIRECTIONS

1. Add all ingredients, except salmon, in a bowl. Whisk for about 2 minutes.

2. Brush both pieces of salmon with teriyaki sauce. Coat both pieces very well.

3. Bake in a 400-degree oven for about 15–18 minutes, occasionally brushing salmon with sauce.

INGREDIENTS

- 2 1-lb. pieces of fresh salmon (bones removed, if any)
- ¼ cup sesame oil
- ¼ cup soy sauce
- 2 tbs. brown sugar
- 1 tsp. ground ginger
- ¼ tsp. garlic powder

GRILLED TUNA WITH SAUTÉED CHICKPEAS AND SUN-DRIED TOMATOES

DIRECTIONS

1. Sprinkle a pinch of sea salt and ground black pepper on tuna.

2. With a little olive oil, brush a heated grill. Grill tuna until desired taste.

3. In a skillet, put 2 tbs. of olive oil. Heat for 1 minute and add chickpeas, red onions, carrots, and sun-dried tomatoes.

4. Sprinkle with a pinch of sea salt and ground black pepper. Mix well.

5. After 3 minutes, add white balsamic vinegar. Cook for 1 additional minute.

6. Pour over grilled tuna and serve hot.

INGREDIENTS

- 1 lb. piece of fresh tuna
- 1 cup canned chickpeas (drained)
- ¼ cup red onion (chopped)
- ½ cup fresh carrots (chopped)
- ¼ cup sun-dried tomatoes in olive oil (chopped)
- sea salt and ground black pepper
- 2 tbs. olive oil plus a little extra
- 1 tbs. dry white wine vinegar

SAUTÉED SHRIMP WITH RADICCHIO, ENDIVE, AND CANDIED PECANS

DIRECTIONS

1. Put uncooked shrimp and dry white wine in a ziplock bag and refrigerate for at least 3 hours.

2. In a skillet, put 2 tbs. of olive oil. Add 2 cloves of chopped garlic and brown. When garlic has browned, add shrimp. Sprinkle with sea salt and ground black pepper. Stir and turn shrimp for about 4 minutes. Shrimp should be pink. Remove and put to the side.

3. In the same skillet, pour 2 tbs. of olive oil and remaining garlic. Brown garlic. When garlic is browned, add shredded radicchio and endive. Add a drop of olive oil and a little sea salt and ground black pepper. Stir occasionally (approximately 5 minutes). Add pecans. Stir.

4. When radicchio and endive are tender, add shrimp. Cook for 1 additional minute and serve.

INGREDIENTS

- 1 ½ lbs. of shrimp (tails removed)
- 2 cups dry white wine (Moscato or a Riesling)
- 3 heads radicchio
- 3 heads endive
- 1 cup whole candied pecans
- 4 garlic cloves (chopped)
- 4 tbs. olive oil plus a little extra
- Sea salt and ground black pepper

SEARED SCALLOPS OVER LENTILS TOPPED WITH GRILLED ZUCCHINI

DIRECTIONS

1. In a large pan, put 1 tbs. of olive oil. Add ½ of the garlic. Brown for a minute and add lentils. Stir. Add 1 tsp. of sea salt. Cook for 4 minutes and remove.

2. Put lentils in a food processor and blend until creamy. Put in a pan and keep warm.

3. In another pan, put 1 tbs. of olive oil and sauté thinly sliced zucchini until tender or a little crunchy. Remove and keep warm.

4. In a large skillet, put 2 tbs. of olive oil and remaining garlic. Brown garlic and add scallops. Cook scallops on each side for about 4 minutes each. Right before scallops are done, put lemon over scallops. Sprinkle with 1 tsp. of sea salt and ½ tsp. of ground black pepper. Stir for a minute.

5. To serve, put a layer of lentils on a plate and spread it out. Put scallops on top. Put pieces of zucchini on top.

INGREDIENTS

- 1 ½ lbs. sea scallops
- 2 10-oz. cans lentils (drained)
- 1 large zucchini (thinly sliced) (see photo)
- 4 tbs. olive oil
- 1 lemon (juiced)
- 2 garlic cloves (chopped)
- 2 tsp. sea salt
- ½ tsp. ground black pepper

MUSSELS MARINARA

DIRECTIONS

1. In a large, deep pot, with a cover, put olive oil and garlic. Brown garlic for 1 minute and add crushed tomatoes. Add sea salt, basil, and stir.

2. On medium heat, cooked crushed tomatoes for about 10 minutes. Stir frequently.

3. After 10 minutes, add mussels to the pot. Stir them around in the sauce

4. Put a cover on the pot and cook on a medium heat.

5. After 5 minutes, remove lid. Mussels should have opened. Stir mussels again in the sauce.

6. Let cook for another 3 minutes and serve.

7. Serve hot.

INGREDIENTS

- 3 lbs. mussels (cleaned)
- 2 12-oz. cans crushed tomatoes
- 3 garlic cloves (chopped)
- 4 basil leaves (chopped)
- 3 tbs. olive oil
- 1 tsp. sea salt

PASTA

LINGUINE WITH SHRIMP AND OLIVES

DIRECTIONS

1. Remove tails from shrimp. Boil for 4–5 minutes and drain well.

2. Add shrimp to your tomato sauce.

3. Boil linguine for 10 minutes or to desired taste. Drain well.

4. Heat sauce and shrimp.

5. Put shrimp and some sauce on top of linguine.

6. Pour olives and cherry tomatoes over linguine. Mix well.

7. Put grated Parmesan cheese on top.

8. Serve hot.

INGREDIENTS

- 1 lb. linguine
- 1 lb. shrimp (thawed)
- 1 cup cherry tomatoes (room temperature)
- 1 cup assorted olives in olive oil (room temperature; pitted is better)
- 2 cups tomato sauce
- ¼ cup Parmesan cheese (grated)

COLD RAVIOLI SALAD

DIRECTIONS

1. Boil ravioli. Time will depend on size of ravioli. After boiling, drain ravioli well. Let cool for about 5 minutes.

2. In a large bowl, add raviolis, all peppers, and red onions. Add olive oil, balsamic vinegar, sea salt, and ground black pepper. Stir gently and mix well.

3. Refrigerate up to 3 hours and then serve.

INGREDIENTS

- 1 lb. small baby ravioli
- 2 red peppers (cut into bite-size pieces)
- 1 green pepper (cut into bite-size pieces)
- 1 orange pepper (cut into bite-size pieces)
- 1 red onion (chopped)
- 5 tbs. olive oil
- 3 tbs. balsamic vinegar
- sea salt and ground black pepper (pinch of each)

PENNE POMODORO

YOU WILL ADD YOUR COOKED PASTA TO THIS TASTY SAUCE.

DIRECTIONS

1. Heat a skillet over medium-high heat. Add olive oil.

2. Add the onion and garlic, and cook for 2 minutes.

3. Add tomatoes and cook, tossing for 5–7 minutes, or until they have broken down.

4. Add a pinch of sea salt.

5. Add cooked pasta to tomato sauce skillet. Add basil and toss together.

6. Finish with an extra drizzle of olive oil and Parmesan cheese.

INGREDIENTS

- 2 tbs. olive oil
- 2 garlic cloves (chopped)
- 1 medium onion (diced)
- 3 ripe large tomatoes (chopped)
- ¼ cup basil leaves (chopped)
- 1 lb. pasta (cooked)
- ¼ cup Parmesan cheese
- sea salt

SPAGHETTI PIE WITH RICOTTA, MOZZARELLA, AND PEPPERONI

OPTIONAL: IF YOU HAVE A CAST-IRON PAN, YOU CAN BAKE IT IN THE OVEN. BAKE AT 350 DEGREES FOR ABOUT 35—40 MINUTES.

DIRECTIONS

1. Boil spaghetti to desired taste. Drain and pour cold water over spaghetti. Drain well.

2. In a large bowl, mix ricotta, mozzarella, pepperoni, a pinch of sea salt, and ground black pepper. Mix well.

3. Mix the beaten egg into the cooled spaghetti. In a large frying pan, pour olive oil. Put half the spaghetti in pan. Add all ricotta, mozzarella, and pepperoni mixture on top. Spread it out.

4. Put remaining spaghetti on top.

5. On medium heat, cook on 1 side for about 10 minutes. After 8–10 minutes, using a dish, flip over and put back in pan. Cook on other side for another 8–10 minutes. You want it to be crispy on the outside (see picture).

6. Serve hot.

YOU CAN MAKE SMALLER INDIVID-
UAL PIES IN A SMALL FRYING PAN.

INGREDIENTS

- 1 lb. cooked spaghetti
- 1 ½ cups fresh ricotta
- 1 ½ cup fresh mozzarella (shredded)
- 1 cup pepperoni (thinly sliced)
- 2 eggs (beaten)
- 4 tbs. olive oil
- sea salt and ground black pepper

COLD LINGUINE SALAD

DIRECTIONS

1. In a large pot of water, boil linguine for 10–12 minutes.

2. Drain linguine well. Add 1 tbs. of olive oil, garlic, and stir. Add a pinch of sea salt and ground black pepper. Mix well.

3. Add peppers, onion, broccoli, and zucchini. Refrigerate pasta.

4. When ready to serve, remove from refrigerator and add Parmesan cheese. Stir well.

INGREDIENTS

- 1 lb. linguine
- 1 red pepper (sliced thin)
- 1 yellow pepper (sliced thin)
- 1 small red onion (sliced thin)
- 1 head of broccoli (chopped into small pieces)
- 1 zucchini (chopped into bite-size pieces)
- olive oil
- 1 garlic clove (chopped)
- sea salt and ground black pepper
- ¼ cup Parmesan cheese

STUFFED SPINACH RICOTTA SHELLS

DIRECTIONS

1. Preheat oven to 400 degrees.

2. Boil pasta shells according to box directions. Drain well.

3. In a large bowl, add ricotta cheese, ¾ lb. of mozzarella cheese, Parmesan cheese, egg, and spinach. Mix well.

4. In a large baking pan, coat the bottom with tomato sauce.

5. Begin to stuff each pasta shell. Place in pan.

6. Put tomato sauce on top of pasta shells and spread remaining ¼ lb. of shredded mozzarella cheese on top.

7. Bake in oven for 15 minutes. You want cheese melted and bubbly.

INGREDIENTS

- 1 lb. box macaroni shells (for stuffing)
- 1 lb. ricotta cheese
- 1 egg
- 1 cup grated Parmesan cheese
- 1 lb. piece of mozzarella cheese (shredded)
- 2 cups fresh spinach (chopped)
- tomato sauce

PENNE WITH SALAMI AND CARROTS

DIRECTIONS

1. Boil pasta in water until desired taste.

2. In a skillet, add oil and garlic. When garlic browns, add carrots and sun-dried tomatoes. Add a pinch of sea salt and ground black pepper. Cook on a low heat until carrots are tender.

3. Drain pasta. Pour carrot mixture on top. Add salami and sprinkle with Parmesan cheese.

INGREDIENTS

- 1 lb. bow tie pasta
- ½ lb. carrots (shredded)
- 1 cup sun-dried tomatoes in olive oil (chopped)
- ¼ lb. salami (sliced into thin pieces) *at room temperature
- 3 cloves of garlic (chopped)
- 3 tbs. olive oil
- sea salt and ground black pepper
- Parmesan cheese (optional)

CRANBERRY CHICKPEA PENNE

SPRINKLE SOME PARMESAN CHEESE ON TOP.

DIRECTIONS

1. Boil pasta to your desired consistency. Drain well when done.

2. Meanwhile, in a large skillet, put 2 tbs. olive oil. Brown garlic for 1 minute and then add chickpeas, peas, cranberries, sea salt, and ground black pepper.

3. Stir well. Cook for about 5 minutes. Then add 1 tbs. of olive oil, red wine vinegar, and sugar. Stir.

4. Cook for 1 additional minute and pour over pasta.

INGREDIENTS

- 1 lb. pasta (ziti goes well with this recipe)
- 1 10-oz. can chickpeas (drained and rinsed)
- 1 cup fresh peas
- 1 cup dried cranberries
- 2 garlic cloves (chopped)
- 3 tbs. olive oil
- 2 tbs. red wine vinegar
- 1 tsp. sea salt
- ½ tsp. ground black pepper
- 1 tsp. sugar
- Parmesan cheese (optional)

PENNE WITH MUSHROOMS AND SUN-DRIED TOMATOES

DIRECTIONS

1. Boil mushrooms for 5 minutes and drain well. Leave to the side.

2. In a large pot of boiling water, boil pasta to desired taste (between 10–12 minutes).

3. In a large skillet, add olive oil. Brown garlic for 3 minutes. Add mushrooms, sun-dried tomatoes, pignoli nuts (optional), and basil. Add a pinch of sea salt and ground black pepper. Stir together.

4. Drain pasta well. Pour tomato-mushroom mixture on top. Sprinkle Parmesan cheese on top.

5. Serve hot.

INGREDIENTS

- 1 lb. penne
- 1 lb. white button mushrooms (sliced)
- 1 cup sun-dried tomatoes in oil (chopped)
- ½ cup pine nuts (pignoli nuts) (optional)
- 1 tbs. basil (washed and chopped)
- 4 garlic cloves (chopped)
- 3 tbs. olive oil
- sea salt and ground black pepper
- ¼ cup Parmesan cheese

GNOCCHI WITH A RED WINE TOMATO SAUCE

DIRECTIONS

1. Peel potatoes and place them in a steamer for about 30–40 minutes, or until tender.

2. Use a potato ricer to mash potatoes.

3. Add sea salt to the flour; then add some flour to the potatoes to absorb the water.

4. Put potatoes on a floured board and use your hands to mix in the remaining flour.

5. Knead the flour and potatoes until it forms firm dough.

6. Form some of the dough into a ball and roll into a long rope.

7. Cut into 1-inch pieces and press lightly with a fork.

8. Place the potato gnocchi in a large pot of salted boiling water. When the gnocchi floats to the top, remove the potato gnocchi with a slotted spoon (about 2 minutes). Pour sauce (recipe below) over gnocchi.

SAUCE INGREDIENTS

- 2 lbs. plum tomatoes (peeled, seeded, and chopped)
- 1 medium-sized yellow onion (chopped)
- 3 garlic cloves (chopped)
- 4 leaves of fresh basil
- ¼ cup fresh parsley (chopped)
- 3 tbs. tomato paste
- ½ cup of dry red wine
- 2 tbs. olive oil
- 1 tsp. dry oregano

INGREDIENTS

- 2 lbs. yellow potatoes
- 2 cups all-purpose flour
- 2 tsp. sea salt

VEGETABLES

BROCCOLI-STUFFED POTATO SKINS

DIRECTIONS

1. Preheat oven to 400 degrees.

2. Bake potatoes for 45 minutes or until soft. Let cool and cut in half. Scoop out the inside.

3. In a large bowl, add potatoes and all ingredients. Mix well.

4. Stuff potatoes and drizzle 1 drop of olive oil on top of each potato.

5. Put stuffed potato skins on baking pan and return to oven for 10–12 minutes. Cheese should be melted and bubbly (see photo). Serve hot.

INGREDIENTS

- 1 lb. of broccoli (boiled until tender and drained well; then chop broccoli)
- 6 large baking potatoes (russet potatoes)
- 1 cup mozzarella cheese (shredded)
- 1 cup cheddar cheese (shredded)
- 1 tsp. sea salt
- ½ tsp. ground black pepper
- 2 tbs. olive oil

CHEESE AND SPINACH PORTOBELLO MUSHROOMS

DIRECTIONS

1. Preheat oven to 400 degrees.

2. Steam portobello mushrooms for 5 minutes, or until tender.

3. In a deep baking pan, brush 1 tbs. of olive oil. Put steamed mushrooms in pan.

4. In a bowl, mix all ingredients with 3 tbs. of olive oil. Mix well.

5. Stuff each mushroom with spinach mixture.

6. Bake in oven for 6–8 minutes. Cheese should be melted and bubbly.

7. Serve hot.

INGREDIENTS

- 4 large portobello mushrooms (rinsed and dried of excess water)
- 1 cup fresh spinach (chopped)
- ½ cup sweet onion (minced)
- 1 garlic clove (minced)
- ½ cup white cheddar cheese (shredded)
- ¼ cup Romano cheese (grated)
- ½ tsp. sea salt
- ½ tsp. ground black pepper
- 4 tbs. olive oil

SPINACH AND BLACK BEANS WITH PECANS

YOU CAN USE WALNUTS INSTEAD OF PECANS.

DIRECTIONS

1. Remove stems and rinse spinach in strainer. Shake out all the water.

2. In a large skillet, sauté 2 cloves of chopped garlic with about 2 tbs. of olive oil. When garlic is beginning to brown, throw in spinach. Season (sprinkle) with sea salt and ground black pepper. Drizzle with a bit of olive oil.

3. Stir occasionally. Process takes about 5 minutes. In a smaller skillet, add remaining garlic with a tbs. of olive oil.

4. As garlic browns, add black beans and pecans. Season (sprinkle) with sea salt and ground black pepper, and add a drop of olive oil and stir. Cook for 3 minutes.

5. Pour spinach into a serving bowl. Pour black bean and pecan mixture on top.

6. Serve warm.

INGREDIENTS

- 1 ½ lbs. fresh spinach
- 3 garlic cloves (chopped)
- 4 tbs. olive oil plus extra, if needed
- 1 15.5-oz. can of black beans (drained and rinsed)
- ¾ cup whole pecans
- sea salt and ground black pepper

BRUSSELS SPROUTS WITH BACON AND ALMONDS

BRUSSELS SPROUTS SHOULD BE TENDER YOU CAN SQUEEZE A LITTLE LEMON ON TOP, IF YOU LIKE.

DIRECTIONS

1. Rinse Brussels sprouts. Cut in half. If large, cut in quarters.

2. In a skillet, cook bacon until crispy and put to the side.

3. In a skillet, add 3 tbs. of olive oil. Add garlic. When garlic begins to brown, add Brussels sprouts. Sprinkle a pinch of sea salt and ground black pepper. Add an extra tbs. of olive oil if it appears dry. Stir often so the Brussels sprouts don't burn. After 5 minutes, add vegetable stock. Let simmer on low heat until stock evaporates. Stir frequently.

4. When Brussels sprouts are tender, add chopped cooked bacon into pieces and add to Brussels sprouts. Add sliced almonds and stir. Cook for additional 3 minutes and serve.

INGREDIENTS

- 1 lb. Brussels sprouts
- 3 garlic cloves (chopped)
- 1 cup unsalted almonds (sliced)
- 8 slices of bacon (cooked)
- 2 cups of vegetable stock
- 3 tbs. olive oil plus extra, if needed
- sea salt and ground black pepper

ROASTED CARROTS

SQUEEZE FRESH LEMON ON TOP 5 MINUTES BEFORE REMOVING FROM OVEN.

DIRECTIONS

1. Preheat oven to 400°F.

2. Line a roasting pan with aluminum foil. Place the carrots, red onion wedges, and crushed garlic cloves on the pan and sprinkle with chopped rosemary.

3. Drizzle with olive oil and toss to combine so that the carrots and onions are lightly coated. Sprinkle with sea salt and ground black pepper.

4. Roast at 400 for 30–40 minutes, or until well browned and caramelized around the edges. Remove from pan and place in a serving dish to serve.

INGREDIENTS

- 1 ½ lbs. of fresh carrots (rinsed and cleaned well; patted dry; leave an inch of the green stem on)
- 1 large red onion (cut into small wedges)
- 3 tbs. olive oil
- 1 tbs. fresh rosemary (chopped)
- 2 garlic cloves (peeled and crushed)
- sea salt and ground black pepper

GRILLED STACKED VEGETABLES

DIRECTIONS

1. Preheat oven to 350 degrees.

2. Brush all vegetables with olive oil and sprinkle with sea salt.

3. Grill all vegetables until tender. Set to the side.

4. Begin to stack vegetables and mozzarella: eggplant, zucchini, mozzarella, roasted pepper, eggplant, zucchini, and mozzarella on top.

5. In a food processor, place 3 tbs. of olive oil and basil. Beat for 1 minute. Drizzle olive oil on top of cheese.

6. Put a little olive oil in a baking pan. Put all stacked vegetables in pan.

7. Bake in oven for about 15 minutes, or until heated through and cheese is melted.

INGREDIENTS

- 2 large eggplants (skin removed; sliced ¼ inch thick)
- 2 large zucchinis (sliced ¼ inch thick)
- 3 large red bell peppers (sliced ¼ inch thick)
- 1 ½ lb. piece fresh mozzarella (sliced thin)
- 6 pieces fresh basil
- 3 tbs. olive oil plus extra for brushing vegetables
- sea salt

FRIED STRING BEANS

DIRECTIONS

1. Boil string beans for 3 minutes in boiling water. Drain well. Let cool.

2. Dip string beans in egg, breadcrumbs, and then grated cheese. Cover completely.

3. In a deep fry pan, pour vegetable oil.

4. Heat oil. When it starts to bubble on the sides, add string beans. You can fry them in batches.

5. Cook for about 3–5 minutes, or until they are golden brown. Remove with a strainer and drain on paper towels.

6. Serve warm.

DIPPING SAUCE RECOMMENDATION

- 1 cup of ranch dressing
- 1 tsp. fresh wasabi
  (2 tsp. if you like it spicy)
- Mix together in a bowl. Keep cold
  until serving.

INGREDIENTS

- 1 lb. fresh string beans (ends trimmed)
- 2 cups breadcrumbs
- 1 cup grated Parmesan cheese
- 4 eggs (beaten)
- 2 cups vegetable oil

VEGETABLE FOCACCIA

DIRECTIONS

1. Preheat oven to 350 degrees.

2. Slice all vegetables into thin slices. Put vegetables in a bowl. Pour in olive oil and add a pinch of sea salt and ground black pepper. Mix well.

3. Put all vegetables in a baking pan and bake in oven for approximately 15 minutes. Since vegetables are sliced thin, they should cook quickly. If not, cook a little longer, or until vegetables are tender. *If vegetables appear dry, drizzle a little more olive oil on top.

4. Remove from oven and put vegetables in a bowl. Add balsamic vinegar and garlic. Stir gently, not tearing vegetable slices.

5. Place slices of focaccia bread on a baking pan. Drizzle a drop of olive oil on each slice. Sprinkle a pinch of garlic powder on each slice (optional). Sprinkle a pinch of sea salt and ground black pepper on each slice.

6. Drain vinegar from vegetables. Put slices of each vegetable on each piece of bread. Top with the red onions.

7. Return to oven for 10–12 minutes, or until bread becomes a little crispy.

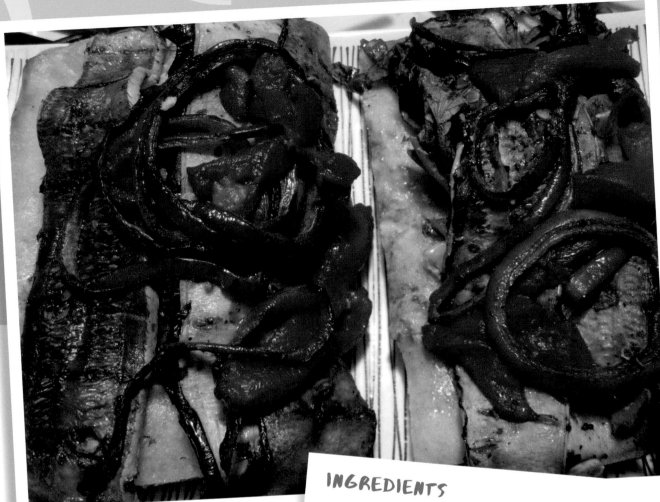

INGREDIENTS

- 1 large green zucchini
- 1 large yellow zucchini
- 1 large eggplant (peeled)
- 2 large red peppers
- 1 large red onion
- 2 garlic cloves (chopped)
- ¼ cup of olive oil
- ¼ cup of balsamic vinegar
- sea salt and ground black pepper
- garlic powder (optional)
- focaccia bread

STUFFED ZUCCHINI

DIRECTIONS

1. Preheat oven to 350 degrees.

2. In a skillet, add 3 tbs. of olive oil. Cook scooped out zucchini, carrots and onions for 5 minutes.

3. Add cooked rice, Parmesan cheese, sea salt, ground black pepper, parsley, and tomato sauce to skillet. Stir well. Let cook for 3 minutes. Let cool for 10 minutes.

4. Stuff zucchini halves with rice stuffing. Pack the rice well into each piece.

5. In a greased baking pan, coated with 2 tbs. of olive oil, place the zucchini pieces rice side up.

6. Bake in oven for about 15–20 minutes. You want the zucchini to be tender, but not too soft.

7. Serve hot.

INGREDIENTS

- 6 medium sized zucchinis (cut in half length wise and scoop out inside; see photo)
- 2 cups cooked brown rice
- 2 large carrots (diced)
- 1 sweet onion (chopped)
- ½ cup Parmesan cheese
- ¾ cup tomato sauce
- 1 tsp. fresh parsley (chopped)
- ½ tsp. sea salt
- ½ tsp. ground black pepper
- 5 tbs. olive oil

STUFFED CHEDDAR POTATO MUSHROOMS

DIRECTIONS

1. Preheat oven to 400 degrees.

2. Boil cubed potatoes until tender (about 15 minutes). Drain when done.

3. In a large bowl, place potatoes, cheddar cheese, butter, cream, sea salt, pepper, and parsley. Mix together until creamy.

4. Clean all mushrooms and dry each one. Stuff each mushroom with potato mixture.

5. In a deep baking pan, place stuffed mushrooms. Pour vegetable stock into pan. Do not let stock touch top of potatoes. Vegetable stock should cover the mushrooms halfway.

6. Bake in oven for about 12–15 minutes, or until mushrooms are tender and potatoes are browned on top.

7. Serve hot.

INGREDIENTS

- 16–20 large stuffing mushrooms
- 6 large potatoes (peeled and cubed)
- 1 cup sharp white cheddar cheese (shredded)
- 1 ½ tsp. sea salt
- ½ tsp. ground black pepper
- ½ stick unsalted butter (melted)
- ½ cup heavy cream (plus a little extra if needed)
- 2 tbs. fresh parsley (chopped)
- 2 cups vegetable stock

CREAMY GARLIC PARSNIPS
(A WONDERFUL ALTERNATIVE TO MASHED POTATOES)

DIRECTIONS

1. Wash, peel, and cut parsnips into cubes. Place into boiling water for approximately 30 minutes, or until parsnips can be picked up with a fork.

2. Meanwhile, take 1 whole garlic bulb. Put 1 tbs. of olive oil on the bulb and wrap in aluminum foil. Place in a 400-degree oven for 30 minutes. You want the garlic bulbs to be soft when done.

3. After 30 minutes, strain parsnips and remove garlic from oven and remove skin.

4. In a mixing bowl, add parsnips, cream cheese, heavy cream, garlic, sea salt, and ground black pepper. With a mixer, mix parsnips until creamy. Add a little extra sea salt and ground black pepper, if needed.

5. Serve warm.

INGREDIENTS

- 2 lbs. parsnips
- 8 oz. cream cheese
- ½ cup heavy cream
- 1 garlic bulb
- 2 tsp. sea salt
- 1 tsp. ground black pepper
- 1 tbs. olive oil

CARROTS WITH CRANBERRIES AND WALNUTS

DIRECTIONS

1. In a large skillet, pour 3 tbs. of olive oil. Brown garlic for 1 minute and then add carrots. Stir well.

2. Add 1 tsp. of sea salt and stir. Stir frequently so carrots don't burn. If it seems a little dry, add another tbs. or 2 of olive oil.

3. When carrots become tender, add cranberries, walnuts, and 1 tsp. of sea salt. Stir.

4. Cook for an additional 3–4 minutes.

5. Serve hot.

INGREDIENTS

- 1 ½ lbs. carrots (thinly sliced sticks)
- 1 cup dried cranberries
- 1 cup of walnuts (cut into pieces)
- 3 garlic cloves (chopped)
- 2 tsp. sea salt
- 3 tbs. olive oil

DESSERT

PUMPKIN WHOOPIE PIES

DIRECTIONS

1. Preheat the oven to 350 degrees.

2. Line 2 baking sheets with parchment paper.

3. In a large bowl, mix 1 tsp. of vanilla, melted butter, and brown sugar until smooth. Add eggs, pumpkin puree, pumpkin pie spice, vanilla, baking powder, and baking soda. Using a rubber spatula, add flour and mix in gently.

4. Using a tablespoon, drop 12 tbs. of batter, spaced evenly, onto each baking sheet. Bake for about 10–12 minutes. Use a toothpick to make sure it's dry inside. Put on a rack to cool.

5. Meanwhile, using an electric mixer, cream the softened butter with the cream cheese. Add confectioners' sugar, ½ tsp. of vanilla, and mix on low speed until blended. Beat until fluffy.

6. Spread cream cheese on one half and put other half on top.

7. Keep refrigerated. Take out 15 minutes before serving.

INGREDIENTS

- 1 ½ sticks unsalted butter (6 ounces)
  —1 stick melted, ½ stick softened
- 1 cup packed light brown sugar
- 2 eggs (beaten)
- 1 cup canned pumpkin puree
- 1 tbs. pumpkin pie spice
- 1 tsp. vanilla extract
- 1 tsp. baking powder
- 1 tsp. baking soda
- 1 ⅔ cups flour
- 4 ounces cold cream cheese
- 1 cup confectioners' sugar

SUNFLOWER SEED MUFFINS

DIRECTIONS

1. Preheat oven to 350 degrees.

2. Lightly butter a 12-cup muffin tin.

3. Put the orange juice, eggs, honey, and orange zest into a medium bowl and mix well.

4. Mix the flour, oats, baking powder, baking soda, and salt together in a large bowl.

5. Add the orange juice mixture and combine. Use as few strokes as possible so you do not overmix the batter.

6. Spoon the batter into prepared muffin tins. Fill about ¾ full.

7. Sprinkle with sunflower seeds on top.

8. Bake for about 20–25 minutes, or until a toothpick comes out clean when tested.

9. Let the muffins cool before removing them from the pan.

10. Suggestion: serve with a blueberry preserve.

INGREDIENTS

- 1 cup freshly squeezed orange juice
- ⅓ cup butter (for greasing muffin tin)
- ⅓ cup honey
- 3 large eggs
- grated zest of 1 orange
- 2 cups whole grain flour (spelt, kamut, or whole wheat)
- 1 cup rolled oats
- 1 tsp. baking powder
- 1 tsp. baking soda
- ½ tsp. salt
- pumpkin seeds

BLUEBERRY PEACH LATTICE PIE FOR FOURTH OF JULY

DIRECTIONS

1. Preheat oven to 400 degrees.

2. In a food processor, mix all dry piecrust ingredients and then add cold butter. Pulse 6–8 times. Flour should be coarse. Slowly add 1 tbs. of iced water at a time. Pulse slowly. Dough should become firm. Pinch dough, and it should be firm. Add 1 drop of water if it's not firm.

3. Roll dough on a floured surface. Roll into a ball and cut in half.

4. In a large bowl, put peaches, blueberries, sugar, cornstarch, and vanilla extract. Mix together.

5. Take half of the dough and roll out. Place dough in 9-inch pie pan.

6. Take fruit filling and put in pan.

7. Take second half of dough and roll out. Cut dough into 1-inch strips.

8. Crisscross strips of dough on top of pie (see photo). Crimp dough around entire pie.

9. In a little bowl, mix egg white and water.

10. Brush egg wash on top of pie thoroughly. Sprinkle coarse sugar on top of dough strips.

11. Place pie pan on a cookie sheet. You don't want pie juice dripping onto the stove.

12. Bake in oven for about 30 minutes. Reduce heat to 350 degrees and bake for another 20 minutes. Piecrust should be golden brown, and fruit should be bubbly when done.

PIE CRUST INGREDIENTS

- 2 ½ cups all-purpose flour
- 2 sticks of very cold unsalted butter (cut into ¼-inch pieces)
- 1 tsp. sugar
- 1 tsp. salt
- 7 tbs. ice water

INGREDIENTS

- 4 cups of fresh peaches (peeled and sliced)
- 1 pint of fresh blueberries (rinsed and drained; all stems removed)
- ¾ cup granulated sugar
- 1 tsp. vanilla extract
- 2 ½ tsp. cornstarch

EGG WASH AND SUGAR INGREDIENTS

- 1 large egg white (beaten)
- 1 tsp. water
- 1–2 tbs. coarse sugar (for sprinkling)

CHEESECAKE

DON'T OPEN OVEN WHILE BAKING. ONLY OPEN WHEN OVEN HAS COMPLETELY COOLED DOWN.

DIRECTIONS

1. Mix all ingredients together. Mix well. Set aside.

CRUST DIRECTIONS

1. Preheat oven to 350 degrees.

2. Mix crust ingredients.

3. In a 9-inch spring pan, layer graham cracker filling on the bottom of the pan. Make sure crumbs are spread evenly.

4. Pour cream cheese mixture on top of crumbs.

5. Bake for 1 hour. Turn off oven and let cake sit in oven until oven is cool.

6. You can use canned cherries, blueberries, or pineapples on top. You can also leave it plain.

7. Keep refrigerated.

INGREDIENTS

- 4 8-oz. bars of cream cheese (softened)
- 5 eggs
- 1 ½ pints sour cream
- 4 tsp. vanilla extract

INGREDIENTS FOR CRUST

- 1 ½ cups graham cracker crumbs
- ¾ stick margarine
- 3 tbs. sugar

EASTER TURNOVERS

DIRECTIONS

1. Soak raisins in cold water overnight. Drain very well.

2. In a large bowl, add chocolate chips, pine nuts, walnuts, raisins, and orange peel. Stir and mix well. Refrigerate for 30 minutes.

3. To make dough, combine all ingredients and mix well to form dough. Roll out dough to make small circles. You can use the cover of a sugar bowl or a small dish, depending on the size of the turnover.

4. Remove raisin mixture from refrigerator and spoon mixture on each circle. The amount will depend on the size circles you have created. It should be enough, but not too much, where the turnover will break open when you fold it over. Fold the turnover and seal edges with a fork. Place on a greased (about 1 tbs. of butter) baking sheet.

5. Take 1 egg and beat it. Add 1 tbs. of water. Beat again. This is your egg wash. Brush a little on each turnover. This helps the turnover turn golden brown.

6. Bake in oven for 15–18 minutes. Watch so they don't burn. Remove and let cool.

7. Yields about 2 dozen.

INGREDIENTS FOR FILLING

- ½ lb. milk chocolate chips
- ½ lb. pine nuts (pignoli nuts)
- ½ lb. walnuts (chopped)
- 1 box raisins (15 oz.)
- 1 tbs. grated orange peel

INGREDIENTS FOR DOUGH

- 2 cups all-purpose flour
- 1 cup Crisco
- 1 tsp. salt
- ½ cup ice water
- 2 oz. sugar
- 1 tsp. vanilla extract

MAPLE SYRUP AND RED WINE PEARS

DIRECTIONS

1. Place wine, maple syrup, and sugar in a large pot with the cinnamon stick.

2. Bring to a boil. Reduce to a simmer and add pears.

3. Cover pot and cook for about 6 minutes.

4. Turn pears and continue cooking (covered) for an additional 8–10 minutes.

5. Cook until pears are tender.

6. Serve pears with vanilla ice cream or whipped cream. You can spoon the reduced liquid over the pears. You can also eat the pears just the way they are.

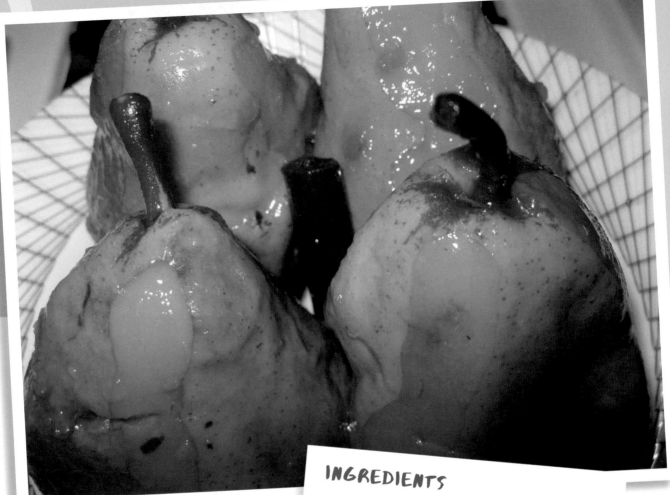

INGREDIENTS

- 2 cups of a light sweet red wine
- 1 cup maple syrup
- ½ cup sugar
- 1 cinnamon stick
- 4 firm pears (peeled and cored)

SESAME SEED COOKIES

DIRECTIONS

1. Preheat oven to 375 degrees.

2. In a mixing bowl, add sugar and margarine. Beat until fluffy. Add eggs, almond extract, and vanilla extract. Stir in flour, baking powder, and salt. Mix well.

3. Roll dough. Cut into 2-inch logs. Dip each log in milk and then in sesame seeds.

4. On a cookie sheet, bake in oven for about 15–20 minutes. Cookies should be a little golden brown.

INGREDIENTS

- 2 ¾ cups flour
- ½ cup soft margarine
- 1 cup of sugar
- 2 eggs
- ½ tsp. baking powder
- ½ tsp. vanilla extract
- ½ tsp. almond extract
- ¼ tsp. salt
- 1 cup of milk
- ½ cups of sesame seeds

THUMBPRINT COOKIES

DIRECTIONS

1. Preheat oven to 350 degrees.

2. In a bowl, with a mixer, stir margarine, sugar, vanilla, and eggs. In a separate bowl, mix flour and baking powder.

3. Add flour mixture to creamed butter mixture and mix together.

4. On a greased cookie sheet, scoop a tablespoon of dough and roll into a ball. Place on cookie sheet. Using your thumb or the back of a teaspoon, press down.

5. Using your favorite preserves (apricot, strawberry, etc.), spoon a little preserve into the center of the cookie dough.

6. Bake 18–20 minutes. Check occasionally to make sure they don't burn on the bottom.

7. Yields about 3 dozen.

INGREDIENTS

- 2 ½ cups all-purpose flour
- 2 sticks of margarine (room temperature)
- 1 ¼ cups sugar
- 2 eggs
- ½ tsp. baking powder
- 2 tsp. of vanilla
- preserves (your choice)

OATMEAL CREAM COOKIES

DIRECTIONS

1. Preheat oven to 350 degrees.

2. In a bowl, place creamed butter, sugar, and brown sugar. Add egg and mix.

3. Add flour, baking soda, cinnamon, and salt. Mix well.

4. Stir in rolled oats, raisins, and walnuts.

5. Drop a tablespoon of batter onto greased cookie sheet. You can make them larger, but smaller is better with cream filling.

6. Bake in oven for 10–12 minutes, or until golden brown.

7. Remove from oven and let cool. You want them to dry a little and be crispy.

CREAM FILLING DIRECTIONS

1. In a bowl, mix cream cheese, confectioners' sugar, and vanilla extract. Mix until creamy. Refrigerate for about 1 hour.

2. Remove from refrigerator and make oatmeal cookie sandwiches with the cookie and cream filling (see photo).

3. Keep cookies refrigerated. Remove cookies from refrigerator 10 minutes before serving.

INGREDIENTS FOR CREAM FILLING

- 2 packages cream cheese (8 oz.)
- 8 oz. box of confectioners' sugar
- 1 ½ tsp. of vanilla extract

INGREDIENTS

- 1 ¼ cups flour
- 1 tsp. baking soda
- ¼ tsp. salt
- ½ tsp. ground cinnamon
- 2 ¾ cups of rolled oats
- 1 cup of walnuts (chopped into small pieces)
- 1 cup of raisins
- ¾ cup margarine or butter (softened)
- ¾ cup of sugar
- ¾ cup light brown sugar
- 2 eggs

PEANUT BUTTER AND JELLY COOKIES

DIRECTIONS

1. Preheat oven to 350 degrees.

2. Combine all ingredients (except jelly) in a bowl. Mix until smooth.

3. Roll into 1-inch balls. Place balls on a nonstick baking pan. Press your thumb into each ball.

4. Bake in oven for 10 minutes and remove.

5. Put a little jelly in each print. Return to oven for 2 minutes and remove.

6. Let cool and serve.

INGREDIENTS

- 1 cup of peanut butter
- ¾ cup sugar
- ¼ cup light brown sugar
- 1 egg
- 1 tsp. vanilla
- ½ cup raspberry, strawberry, or grape jelly (stirred)

CHOCOLATE-COVERED FIGS

KEEP REFRIGERATED.

DIRECTIONS

1. Rinse figs in cold water and dry on paper towels.

2. In a microwave dish, melt chocolate.

3. Dip figs into chocolate and then into sprinkles.

4. Let dry on wax paper.

INGREDIENTS

- 12 fresh figs
- 1 cup of semisweet chocolate morsels
- Sprinkles of various colors

CHOCOLATE CHIP RAISIN COOKIES

DIRECTIONS

1. Preheat oven to 350 degrees.

2. In a bowl, mix flour and baking powder. In another bowl, mix creamed butter, sugar, brown sugar, eggs, and vanilla together.

3. Slowly add flour to creamed mixture. Add raisins and chocolate chips and mix well with a wooden spoon.

4. Drop a rounded tablespoon of batter onto a baking pan (ungreased). Bake for 15–17 minutes. Remove from pan and let cool when done.

INGREDIENTS

- 2 ½ cups of flour
- 1 cup of sugar
- ½ cup light brown sugar
- ½ tsp. baking powder
- 1 cup of margarine or butter
- 2 large eggs
- 1 ½ tsp. vanilla
- 1 cup raisins
- 1 cup chocolate chips (semisweet or milk chocolate)

ABOUT THE AUTHOR

John Contratti has been an elementary school teacher for over thirty years. He's the author of the children's books *Cooking with Mr. C* and *Mr. C Takes Manhattan*. He has cooked on the Hallmark television series *Mad Hungry with Lucinda Scala Quinn*, which was produced by Martha Stewart. His successful cooking blog, "Cooking with Mr. C." is followed by people from all over the world. With his love for acting, television, and film, he has appeared in the television dramas *The Americans* and *Royal Pains*. He is a supporter of Broadway Cares and Keen Company. Mr. Contratti resides in New York.